W9-BIQ-911

Date: 02/13/12

J 975.939 FUR
Furstinger, Nancy.
Everglades : the largest
marsh in the United States /

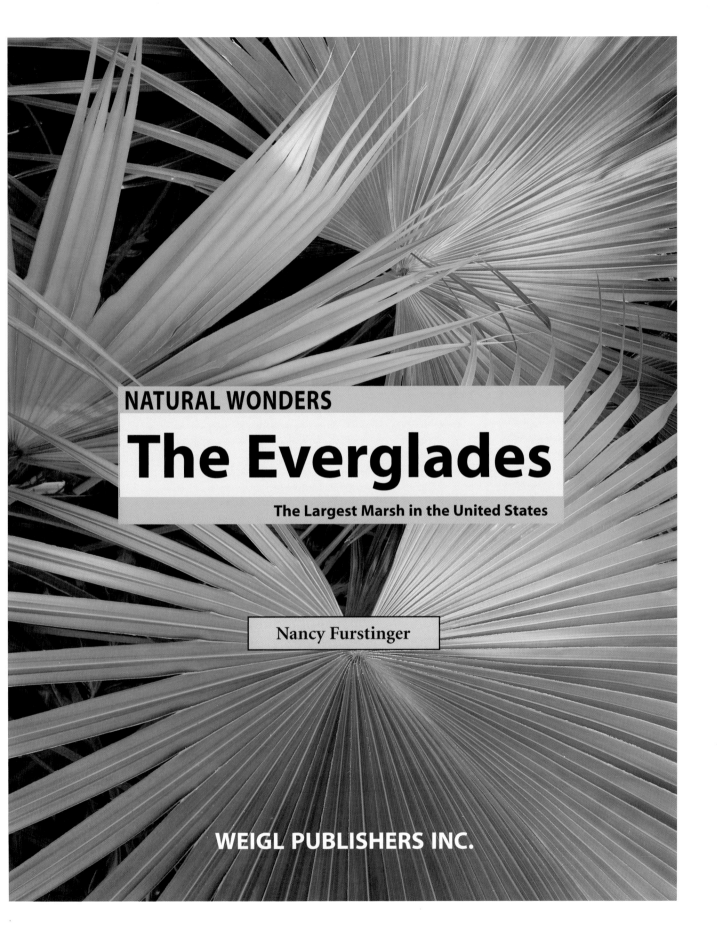

NATURAL WONDERS

The Everglades

The Largest Marsh in the United States

Nancy Furstinger

WEIGL PUBLISHERS INC.

Published by Weigl Publishers Inc.
350 5th Avenue, Suite 3304
New York, NY 10118-0069
USA

Web site: www.weigl.com

Library of Congress Cataloging-in-Publication Data

Furstinger, Nancy.
  Everglades / Nancy Furstinger.
     v. cm. -- (Natural wonders)
  Includes bibliographical references (p.) and index.
  Contents: A river of grass -- A trip back in time -- Where in the
world? --
  Everglades ecosystems -- Endangered Everglades -- A park in danger --
The big
  picture -- People of the Everglades -- A natural heritage -- Must see
and do --
  Key issues : water conflicts -- Timelines -- What have you learned?
     ISBN 1-59036-039-7 (lib. bdg. : alk. paper) – ISBN 1-59036-160-1 (pbk.)
  1. Everglades (Fla.)--Juvenile literature. [1. Everglades (Fla.)] I.
Title. II. Series:
  Natural wonders (Mankato, Minn.)
  F317.E9F87 2003
  975.9'39--dc21
                          2002013590
Printed in the United States of America
1 2 3 4 5 6 7 8 9 0 07 06 05 04 03

Project Coordinators
Michael Lowry
Tina Schwartzenberger

Copy Editor
Frances Purslow

Design
Terry Paulhus

Layout
Virginia Boulay

Photo Researchers
Nicole Bezic King
Wendy Cosh

Contents

A River of Grass

Imagine a river of grass teeming with wildlife. This watery wilderness is the Everglades. It is the largest **marsh** in the United States. Everglades National Park was the first national park dedicated to protect wildlife. It is the only **subtropical** preserve in North America and the only everglades in the world.

The Everglades began to form at the end of the last **Ice Age**, about 10,000 years ago. As the ice melted, a shallow sea flooded the southern part of Florida.

Today, the Everglades is a popular place for tourists to visit. If visitors are lucky, they might spot a rare species, such as the Florida panther or the West Indian manatee.

▬ **Everglades National Park spans the southern tip of Florida.**

Everglades Facts

- The Everglades includes 5,000 square miles of land and water—about the same size as the state of Connecticut.

- The average width of the Everglades is 50 miles. The average depth of the water is only 6 inches.

- More than 400 species of birds have been identified within the park.

- The Everglades is the only place in the world where alligators and crocodiles exist together.

- Everglades National Park is the largest national park east of the Rocky Mountains.

- Everglades National Park has been named a World Heritage Site, an International Biosphere Reserve, and a Wetland of International Importance.

The Everglades Locator

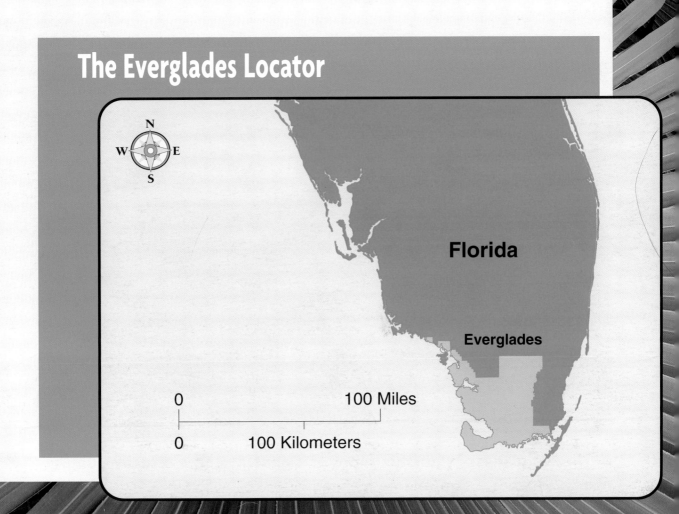

A Trip Back in Time

An ancient sea covered the southern Florida **peninsula** 6 million years ago. The remains of plants and animals on the seafloor slowly turned into limestone. This formed the bedrock of the Everglades. This porous rock is called "egg-stone" because it looks like tiny fish eggs.

Glaciers did not reach southern Florida during the last Ice Age. As the melting ice returned to the sea, however, it helped shape the Everglades. The land was covered by water and dried out four times. Each time the land was covered, more rocks formed.

■ **The Everglades contain thousands of islands. Most are actually clumps of mangrove trees, a tropical tree with many roots.**

Puzzler

Salt water borders much of the Everglades, affecting the community of plants and animals living in southern Florida.

Q From north to south, which U.S. states border the Atlantic Ocean on the East Coast, and which border the Pacific Ocean on the West Coast?

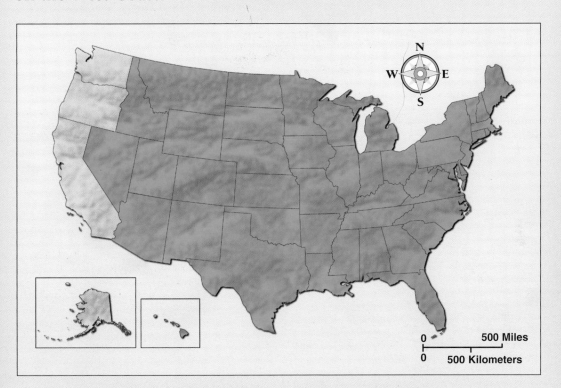

A **East Coast:** Maine, New Hampshire, Massachusetts, Rhode Island, Connecticut, New York, New Jersey, Delaware, Maryland, Virginia, North Carolina, South Carolina, Georgia, Florida

West Coast: Alaska, Washington, Oregon, California

Changing the Flow

For thousands of years, the overflow from Lake Okeechobee has supplied the Everglades with fresh water. Wide but shallow, the Everglades becomes salty as it nears Florida Bay and the Gulf of Mexico. Humans have altered the course of this water flow with more than 1,400 miles of **canals** and **levees**.

During the rainy season—May through September—thunderstorms can dump 12 inches of rain on the Everglades in a single day. Humid summer temperatures can reach 90° Fahrenheit. The hurricane season runs from June through November. December through April is the dry season. Winter temperatures can dip as low as 53°F.

■ As a result of canals and levees, the Everglades contains about half of the water it once did.

River of Sand

An underground river of sand is found above Lake Okeechobee. It extends south under the Everglades and Florida Bay. This sand deposit was worn away from the Appalachian Mountains 3 to 5 million years ago. The sand, called the Long Key Formation, holds fresh water.

Hundreds of keys, or small islands, dot the Florida Bay. These tiny islands formed in the shallow bay waters, which average only 4 to 5 feet deep. Mangrove roots grow in the mud beneath the murky water. **Silt**, trapped among the roots, collects and forms new land.

Everglades Ecosystems

An ecosystem is a community of plants and animals that interacts with its environment. An ecosystem can be as small as a rotting log or as large as an ocean. The community of plants and animals found in the Everglades is affected by the natural changes in this large marsh.

Water has a major effect on life in the Everglades. Plants and animals have adapted to the wet and dry cycles. During the rainy season, the river of **sea grass** turns muddy and then flows.

When the rains cease, water levels drop and the dry season begins. The swampy areas attract snakes, frogs, and turtles. These animals are part of the food chain for alligators, crocodiles, and nesting wading birds.

▬ Alligators like to warm themselves in the Sun. This is called basking.

Habitats of the Everglades

A variety of unique **habitats** can be found within the Everglades's boundaries. A few of them are listed below.

Florida Bay
In Florida Bay, keys and sea grass shelter green sea turtles, schools of fish, hammerhead sharks, and seahorses.

Mangrove Forests
Where fresh water meets salt water, mangrove forests help pink shrimp spawn and house nesting birds.

Coastal Prairie
Inland, on the coastal prairie, desert plants withstand waves and wind.

Fresh Water
Teardrop-shaped tree islands called hammocks grow in freshwater **sloughs**. White-tailed deer munch on nutrient-rich sea grass.

Swamps
Cypress trees grow out of swamps, offering havens for pelicans and roseate spoonbills.

A Park in Danger

In 1934, a special committee convinced Congress to create Everglades National Park. The park would protect endangered birds and safeguard the freshwater and saltwater habitats. When the park was finally created in 1947, President Harry S. Truman said, "The spectacular plant and animal life distinguishes this place from all others in our country."

Today, the Everglades is considered one of the country's most endangered national parks. Mercury poisons the water, fish, and all the animals that depend on fish for their diets. Sea grass is dying off in Florida Bay. Many of these problems are connected to human development. Pollution and a change in the water flow are some of the problems affecting the Everglades.

More than half of the Everglades has been lost to agricultural and housing development.

What Can I Do?

There is no other place in the world like the Everglades. Although it is a protected national park, this does not guarantee the survival of endangered species. Humans have changed the Everglades. Land development, pollution, and changing water flow—all of these activities cause problems for animals. Wherever you live, you can do your part to help.

Conserve water. Do not waste water by letting it run while you wash your hands or brush your teeth. Take short showers instead of baths.

Spread the word by informing your friends about what they can do to help.

When visiting parks, do not feed animals. Never attempt to turn them into pets. Do not pick plants or remove natural objects from parks. Stay on the park trails and avoid making loud noises.

Stop pollution. Never throw trash on the ground or in the water.

Animals on the Brink

Fifteen endangered species call Everglades National Park home. Animals that are in danger of becoming extinct include the 1,000-pound West Indian manatee, or sea cow. These gentle creatures rest just below the water, where they risk being hit by speeding boats.

The American crocodile roams mangrove swamps, eating fish. This reptile's habitat is threatened by human development. The long-legged wood stork is in danger because of water control programs. On land, the Florida panther is fighting for survival. Its habitat is being destroyed. This large brown cat is also at risk of being killed by speeding cars.

Manatees have no natural enemies. Most human-related manatee deaths are from collisions with boats. Manatees are also crushed or drowned in canal locks, ingest fish hooks or litter, and get tangled in crab trap lines.

Biography

Ernest Coe (1866–1951)

As a boy, Ernest Coe enjoyed exploring the outdoors in New Haven, Connecticut. As a landscape architect in Miami, Florida, Coe used plants and trees to decorate gardens and other public and private spaces. When he realized that rare birds in the Everglades were being killed, Coe discovered a new mission. He vowed to preserve the Everglades. Coe created the Tropical Everglades National Park Association in 1928. His efforts spurred interest in the new Everglades park. Nicknamed "Father of the Everglades," Coe loved the tropical beauty of the region.

Facts of Life

Born: March 21, 1866

Hometown: New Haven, Connecticut

Occupation: landscape architect, conservationist

Died: January 1, 1951

The Big Picture

The world can be divided into biomes. Biomes are major natural communities that share similar climates, plants, and animals. One biome is wetlands, such as marshes, swamps, and bogs. Wetlands are a natural link between earth and water. Whether salty or fresh, wetlands filter pollution out of water and prevent floods.

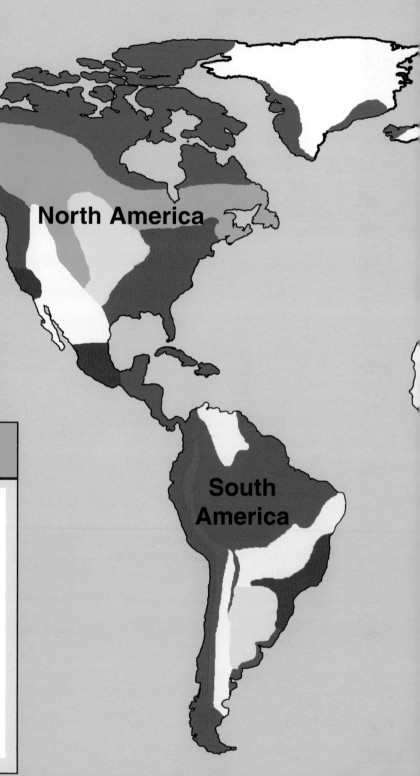

Legend

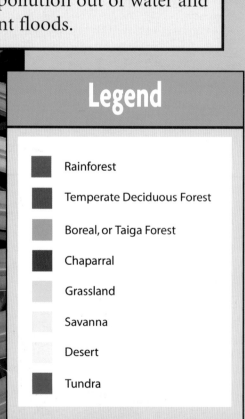

Rainforest

Temperate Deciduous Forest

Boreal, or Taiga Forest

Chaparral

Grassland

Savanna

Desert

Tundra

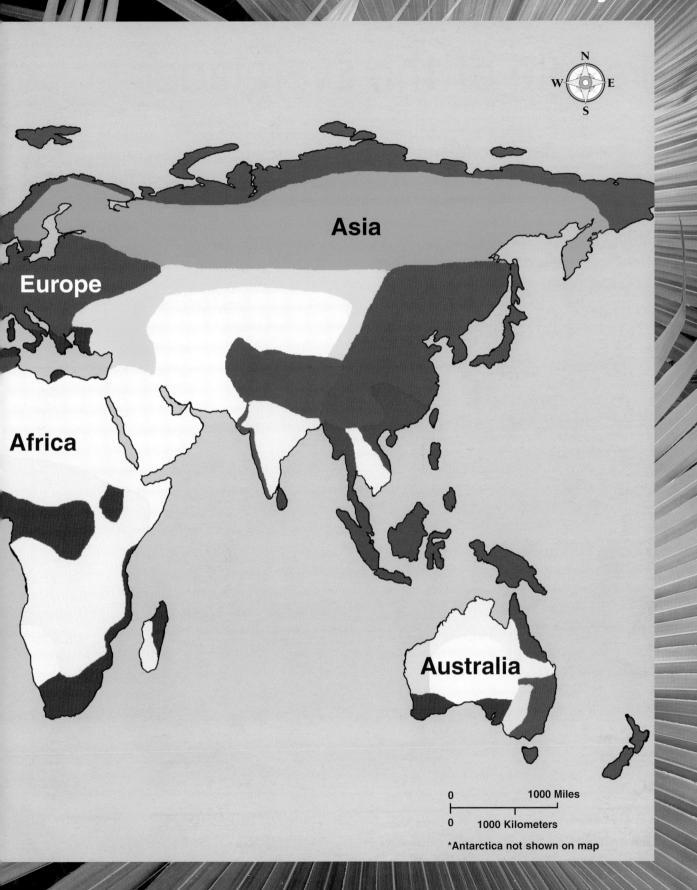

Europe

Asia

Africa

Australia

0 ――――――――― 1000 Miles

0 ――――――――― 1000 Kilometers

*Antarctica not shown on map

People of the Everglades

Paleo-Indians once hunted bison and mammoths in the Everglades region around 10,000 BC. When the wetlands emerged after the climate changed, they began catching shellfish.

When the Spanish arrived in the early 1500s, about 20,000 Native Americans lived in southern Florida. By 1763, when the English gained control of Florida, the Native-American population had shrunk to several hundred. Warfare, slavery, and European diseases, such as smallpox, reduced the Native-American population.

■ During the Seminole Wars in the 1800s, the Seminoles moved to the Everglades to prevent their removal from Florida. Today, the Seminole culture is closely linked to the Everglades.

Puzzler

Early Native Peoples of the Everglades found the resources they needed in nature. They fashioned sharks' teeth into knives and used shells to make fishhooks, picks, hammers, and chisels. These tools were used to carve cypress logs into canoes.

Q Why were shells and sharks' teeth the most practical materials for making tools?

■ **The Seminole people used coconut shells to make rattles.**

A The Native Peoples of the Everglades could find these materials nearby.

A Natural Heritage

Nature has influenced the arts and culture of the Everglades region. Pieces of clay pottery that have been found show early peoples' skill with natural materials. Huge shell mounds mark sites where villages were once located. The early peoples piled up oyster and whelk shells as sites for sacred temples and burial sites.

Today, people continue to be inspired by this river of grass. Seminoles create sweetgrass baskets and palmetto fiber husk dolls to sell at powwows. Nature photographers capture the splendor of the Everglades on film.

■ The Seminoles have made sweetgrass baskets for more than sixty years. Wild sweetgrass is hand-picked from high, dry areas of the Everglades basin, laid in the Sun to dry, and sewn together with colorful threads.

Everglades Mythology

Seminole children have long gathered to listen to campfire legends. In Seminole **mythology**, the Creator, the Grandfather of all things, selected the panther as the first being to walk on Earth. The Creator admired the large cat for its beauty, patience, and strength. He sealed up all of the creatures in a large shell. When the shell cracked, the panther leapt out first. He called the panther *Coo-wah-chobee*, meaning "crawls on four legs close to the ground."

The Creator placed the animals into clans, or groups. Today, Seminoles are members of one of eight clans: Bear, Bigtown, Bird, Deer, Otter, Panther, Snake, and Wind. The Panther clan creates laws and makes medicines.

Natural Attractions

There are countless ways to enjoy the vast beauty of the Everglades. The following are samples of things to see and do.

At Billie Swamp Safari, you can study snakes or watch alligator wrestling. Hop aboard a swamp buggy and head to Sam Jones Camp, where you will learn about the medicine man who led Seminole resistors. Then, sample local food specialties at the Swamp Water Café. Try eating gator nuggets, frog legs, catfish, and fry bread with honey.

Explore the weaving waterways of the 10,000 Islands, where the Everglades meet the sea. Park rangers work as guides on boats, pointing out dolphins, manatees, and birds in the maze of mangroves.

"The Everglades is a test. If we pass it, we get to keep the planet," said environmentalist Joe Podger. Your class might be interested in helping this fragile environment by using the park as an outdoor classroom. Each year more than 10,000 students participate in Everglades National Park's Education Program.

▬ Most national parks host educational programs for school groups. Everglades National Park's Education Program was formed in 1971.

Be Prepared

If you plan to visit the Everglades, even for just an afternoon, it is important to bring supplies with you. To enjoy a safe outing, stay on the trails and keep a careful distance away from all animals.

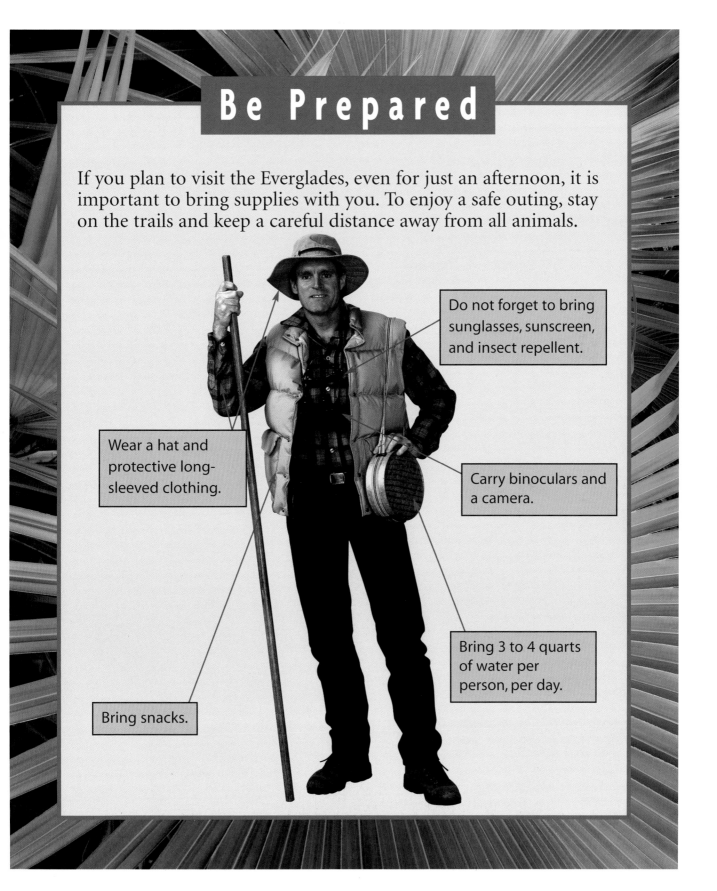

Do not forget to bring sunglasses, sunscreen, and insect repellent.

Wear a hat and protective long-sleeved clothing.

Carry binoculars and a camera.

Bring 3 to 4 quarts of water per person, per day.

Bring snacks.

Water Conflicts

The natural resources of the Everglades face many challenges. Water is at the heart of the problem. Florida's growing population and tourists must share water from the Everglades with endangered wildlife. Since the 1920s, humans have changed the natural flow of water into the park. Canals, pumps, and dikes send water to farms and **urban** areas first. Only then is water used by plants and animals living in the Everglades.

▬ **Farmers in the Everglades Agriculture Area are taking steps to reduce fertilizer runoff.**

In 2000, the government began a thirty-year plan to restore the Everglades. The Comprehensive Everglades Restoration Plan involves removing levees and canals to help restore the natural flow of the river of grass.

Should engineers have altered the flow of water in the Everglades?

YES	NO
Around 900 people requiring 200,000 gallons of fresh water daily move to Florida every day. In addition, 39 million tourists vacationing in Florida make demands on water supplies. There were not enough freshwater sources to supply this demand. It was believed that water from the Everglades should be used.	It is dangerous when people try to control water flow by changing wet and dry seasons. Releasing too much water flooded alligator nests, destroying eggs. Wood storks could not locate enough fish to breed and feed young. Cattail replaced sea grass. Withholding too little water reduced the number of apple snails. As a result, river otters and Everglade kite birds had less to eat.
Water in the Everglades needed to be controlled to help farmers. The wetlands were drained and used for farming and ranching. Fresh water was provided for sugarcane and vegetable fields, citrus farms, dairy farms, and cattle ranches. 	When fresh water runs low, salt water invades the wetlands, upsetting the balance of nature. Runoff from farming fertilizer and chemicals harms the environment, causing problems for Everglades plants and animals. 

Time Line

65 million years ago
Dinosaurs become extinct.

6 million years ago
A shallow sea covers
Big Cypress Swamp
in southern Florida.

**5 million–3 million
years ago**
Sands worn away from
the Appalachian Mountains
are deposited along the
Florida peninsula.

1 million years ago
Glaciers form on all
continents; rocks beneath
the Everglades form.

100,000 years ago
The sea level in southern
Florida rises 100 feet above
modern levels; billions of tiny
coral animals begin forming
the Florida Keys.

10,000–8,000 years ago
Paleo-Indians live in the area,
adapting to new wetlands.

Slash pine is the
dominant plant
in the pinelands
section of the
Everglades. This
area is a dry,
rugged terrain
that sits on top of
a limestone ridge.

The Seminole Stomp Dance is a traditional religious dance.

5,000 years ago
Cypress swamps
and hardwood forests
begin developing.

8,000 BC–750 BC
Early peoples in wetlands
who rely on shellfish create
tools and pottery.

AD 1500–AD 1750
The first Europeans reach
the Everglades.

1763
The English gain control
of Florida from Spain.

1817–1858
During three Seminole Wars,
Native Americans travel to
the Everglades to avoid
being removed from Florida.

1880s
Developers begin digging
drainage canals.

The great white heron is rarely seen outside the Florida Keys or Everglades National Park.

It is illegal to feed alligators in Florida. Alligators lose their fear of humans when people feed them.

1976
Everglades National Park becomes an International Biosphere Reserve and a World Heritage Site.

1978
Everglades National Park becomes a Wilderness Destination.

1986
Scientists begin tracking Florida panthers with electronic equipment.

1987
Everglades National Park becomes a Wetland of International Importance.

1989
Everglades Expansion Act adds East Everglades to the park.

2000
Congress passes the Everglades Restoration Act.

2002
Everglades National Park participates in Entrance Fee-Free Weekend.

1905–1910
Areas of wetlands are transformed into farmland.

1928
Ernest Coe creates the Tropical Everglades National Park Association.

1947
President Harry S. Truman dedicates Everglades National Park.

1948
Congress authorizes the Central and South Florida Project. Roads, canals, levees, and water-control structures are built.

1972–1973
Manatees are protected by the Marine Mammal Protection Act and the Endangered Species Act.

What Have You Learned?

True or False?

Decide whether the following statements are true or false. If the statement is false, make it true.

1. During the last Ice Age, a shallow sea flooded the Everglades.

2. Florida Bay keys are islands of coral rock.

3. The Everglades has both rainy and dry seasons.

4. Since the 1930s, the wading bird population has increased in the park.

5. The Everglades is not an endangered national park.

ANSWERS

1. True
2. False. Florida Bay keys are islands of mangroves.
3. True
4. False. Since the 1930s, the wading bird population has decreased in the park.
5. False. The Everglades is an endangered national park.

Short Answer

Answer the following questions using information from the book.

1. Which two animals can you see together only in the Everglades?
2. When is hurricane season?
3. Who led the fight to preserve the Everglades?
4. What did early Native Peoples of the Everglades use to make tools?
5. Seminoles believe which animal was the first to walk on Earth?

ANSWERS
1. The crocodile and the alligator
2. June through November
3. Ernest Coe
4. Shells
5. The panther

Multiple Choice

Choose the best answer in the following questions.

1. In what state is Everglades National Park?

   a) Georgia
   b) Alabama
   c) Florida
   d) South Carolina

2. The park was first formed to preserve endangered:

   a) birds
   b) alligators
   c) snakes
   d) manatees

3. In what year did Ernest Coe create the Tropical Everglades National Park Association?

   a) 1858
   b) 1928
   c) 1934
   d) 1947

4. These people moved to the Everglades in the 1800s:

   a) the Spanish
   b) the Paleo-Indians
   c) the Pahayokee
   d) the Seminoles

ANSWERS
1. c
2. a
3. b
4. d

Find Out for Yourself

Books

Blaustein, Daniel. *The Everglades and the Gulf Coast.* New York: Benchmark Books, 2000.

Fazio, Wende. *Everglades National Park.* New York: Children's Press, 1999.

Yolen, Jane. *Welcome to the River of Grass.* New York: Putnam Publishing Group, 2001.

Web Sites

Use the Internet to find out more about the people, plants, animals, and water of the Everglades.

National Park Service: The Everglades
www.nps.gov/ever
The National Park Service offers an online travel guide for visiting the Everglades with your class, as well as interesting classroom activities.

Everglades National Park
www.everglades.national-park.com
Whether you are writing an assignment or planning a visit, the Everglades National Park Web site has the information you need.

Seminole Tribe
www.seminoletribe.com/index.shtml
To learn more about the rich culture and history of Native Americans in Florida, visit the Seminole Web site.

Encarta
http://encarta.msn.com
Search this online encyclopedia to find out more about the Everglades.

Skill Matching Page

What did you learn? Look at the questions in the "Skills" column. Compare them to the page number of the answers in the "Page" column. Refresh your memory by reading the "Answer"column below.

SKILLS	ANSWER	PAGE
What facts did I learn from this book?	I learned that the Everglades is nearly the same size as the state of Connecticut.	5
What skills did I learn?	I learned how to read maps.	5, 7, 16–17
What activities did I do?	I answered the questions in the quiz.	28–29
How can I find out more?	I can read the books and visit the Web sites on the Find Out for Yourself page.	30
How can I get involved?	I can help reduce how much water I use. I can also take a trip to the Everglades.	13, 22

Glossary

canals: artificial waterways
habitats: places where plants or animals live and grow
Ice Age: the last period in Earth's history when glaciers covered large areas of the planet
levees: artificial riverbanks built to prevent flooding
marsh: an area of soft, wet land; a border between land and water
mythology: stories about ancient times or natural events
peninsula: a portion of land surrounded by water on three sides
sea grass: a type of grass that rises 3 to 10 feet above the water
silt: fine sand or mud carried by moving water
sloughs: wide, shallow waterways
subtropical: a region bordering the tropical zone
urban: related to the city

Index